Repercu...
from SEXUAL
SINS

The SEXUAL REVOLUTION is wreaking havoc on the family, the Church, and the individual's relationship with Jesus Christ.

FRANK HAMMOND

REPERCUSSIONS FROM SEXUAL SINS

by Frank Hammond

ISBN 10: 0-89228-205-3
ISBN 13: 978-089228-205-0

IMPACT CHRISTIAN BOOKS, INC.
332 Leffingwell Ave., Suite 101
Kirkwood, MO 63122
(314) 822-3309

www.impactchristianbooks.com

All passages are from the **NEW KING JAMES BIBLE** unless otherwise noted.

REPERCUSSIONS FROM SEXUAL SINS

America's sexual revolution is wreaking havoc in the nation, the Church and the family. Promiscuity, nudity and sexual obscenities have become commonplace, and our consciences have become desensitized. No longer is there a widespread outcry against the avalanche of filth flaunted daily before our eyes. We shrug our shoulders over the millions of pornographic sites on the Internet, and the untold casualties that pornography is creating.

The repercussions from sexual sin are mounting as moral convictions falter and sexual fads balloon. Few seem to care or even notice that the homosexual lifestyle has become an acceptable choice, albeit one laced with the killer AIDS virus. Many sexually transmitted diseases are mushrooming throughout the population, especially among teens who have unprotected sex with multiple partners.

As the ranks of unwed mothers grow, an entire generation suffers the consequences in their personalities and lives. As millions of unwanted babies are slaughtered in the womb through abortion, Molech, the god of child sacrifice, is worshipped at the altar of sensual pleasure, the escalating number of abortions becomes a numbing statistic, and hearts are hardened. The divorce rate climbs, even within the Church, and the Church is crippled, becoming less and less effective to insist on true holiness and more and more reluctant to emphasize God's standards of moral purity.

Adultery is commonplace and often applauded. Incest, along with homosexuality, is out of the closet. Sexual abuse is rampant, especially within dysfunctional families. Society seems only mildly cognizant of the wounds caused by unrestrained sex and applies worldly band-aids at great expense with negative results. Condoms are provided, and chastity is scorned. The worldly philosophy can be summed up as, "If it feels good, do it! And don't let it bother your conscience."

Neither a nation nor an individual can escape the consequences of disregarding God's commandments. The Bible warns us that "the wages of sin is death" (Rom. 6:23), and "the way of the transgressors is hard" (Prov. 13:15, KJV). Nevertheless, God's remedy is available when His counsel is heeded: "He who covers his sins will not prosper, but whoever confesses and forsakes them will have mercy" (Prov. 28:13).

BIBLE
TERMINOLOGY

FORNICATION

Fornication (Greek, *porne*) is the principal word used for sexual sin in the New Testament. *Porne*, in its various forms, occurs more than forty times in the New Testament. The King James Bible translates the feminine form of the word as "whore" and the masculine as "whoremonger."

Fornication is used generally in the New Testament to mean "illicit sexual intercourse," including adultery; however, there are a few passages that distinguish fornication as separate from adultery: (see Matt. 15:19; Mark 7:21). There are also a few references where fornication is used in a metaphorical sense to refer to idolatry as spiritual unfaithfulness towards God. (Rev. 14:8; 17:2,4; 18:3).

4

ADULTERY

Adultery [*moicheia*] is unlawful intercourse with the spouse of another. Its prohibition is one of the ten commandments: "You shall not commit adultery" (Exod. 20:14). The tenth commandment also applies, "You shall not covet your neighbor's wife" v. 17.

Jesus taught that for a man to look with lust upon a woman constituted adultery in his heart (Matt. 5:28). Given the right time and opportunity it will find expression. In reference to a young man indulging in secret fornication or adultery, the Bible says,

> Stolen water is sweet, And bread eaten in secret is pleasant. But he does not know that the dead are there, that her guests are in the depths of hell.
>
> Prov. 9:17–18

LUST

Lust (*epithumia*) is another word that pertains to sexual sin. Although sometimes used in a good sense, it generally denotes strong evil desire ready to express itself in bodily activity. What God said to Cain is an example: "... sin lies at the door. And its desire is for you, but you should rule over it" (Gen. 4:7). The KING JAMES sometimes translates *epithumia* as "concupiscence" (Rom 7:8; Col. 3:5; 1 Thess 4:5). It can be rendered "over desire," a desire which goes beyond the boundaries of holiness and conformity to God's laws.

EFFEMINATE

Effeminate (*malakos*) refers to homosexuality.

> Do you not know that the unrighteous will not inherit the kingdom of God? Do not be deceived. Neither **fornicators, nor idolaters, nor adulterers, nor homosexuals** (*malakoi*) nor **sodomites** (*arsenokoites* - lit. "abusers of themselves with mankind; one who lies with a man as with a woman; a catamite

– a boy kept for purposes of sexual perversion)... will inherit the kingdom of God.

1 Cor. 6:9–10 [Brackets mine]

The Greek word translated "effeminate" means "soft to the touch" and is used in the New Testament in reference to clothing; hence, a man who adopts a woman's attire; a transvestite.

Inordinate Affection

Inordinate affection (*pathos*):

> Mortify therefore your members which are upon the earth: **fornication, uncleanness, inordinate affection** (passion, evil concupiscence, and covetousness) which is **idolatry**.
>
> Col. 3:5, KJV [Brackets mine, Emphasis mine]

Pathos describes an affection of the mind or passionate desire which is bad, although not necessarily perverse in a sexual sense. The Greek word means "to suffer," as some are seen to suffer greater sympathy for animals than for humans. It is a prejudiced love. It is an unnatural pity or compassion.

Further, *pathos* can describe a love that is imprudent; an unholy desire; even an erotic love that stimulates sexually. This evil passion sometimes finds expression in bestiality, lying carnally with an animal.

Lasciviousness

Lasciviousness [*aselgeia*] occurs six times in the King James New Testament. Galations 5:19 lists it as a "work of the flesh." The New King James Bible translates the word as "licentiousness" (Eph. 4:19) and the King James Bible refers to those "Who being past feeling have given themselves over unto lasciviousness" (Eph. 4:19). *Aselgeia* denotes excess, unrestrained lust, indecency and wantonness.

Sodomy; Sodomite

Sodomy; sodomite (Heb. *qadesh*). We find it mentioned, for instance, in Deuteronomy:

> "There shall be no whore of the daughters of Israel, nor a **sodomite** of the sons of Israel."
>
> Deut. 23:17, KJV

Sodomy is carnal copulation with a member of the same sex, or with an animal, or unnatural carnal copulation with a member of the opposite sex — as sometimes defiles the marriage bed through oral or anal sex. Sodomy derives its name from the city of Sodom upon which God rained fire and brimstone in judgment upon sodomy. Sodom appears throughout Scripture as a warning example of sin and Divine punishment. Sodomy, common among the Canaanites, is looked upon as an abomination and absolutely prohibited (Lev. 18:22; Deut. 23:17).

Dog

Dog (Heb. *keleb*) is a term applied to prostitutes and sodomites, undoubtedly associated with the shamelessness associated with a dog's perverse behavior.

> "You shall not bring the wages of a harlot or the price of a dog to the house of the Lord your God for any vowed offering, for both of these are an abomination to the Lord your God."
>
> Deut. 23:18

Male and female prostitution was practiced by Baal worshippers in their fertility rites. The earnings of a prostitute are tainted and are not to be offered to pay any vow to the Lord. Whatever is acquired by evil means as well as what is evil in itself is not to be offered to the Lord. Such things do not belong in house of the Lord; nor are they acceptable to Him.

But outside [the Holy City] are dogs and sorcerers and sexually immoral and murderers and idolaters, and whoever loves and practices a lie.

Rev. 22:15 [BRACKETS MINE]

"Dogs" refers generally to those who rebel against the rule of God, whether magicians, unregenerate Gentiles, Judiazers or male prostitutes. Such people will not be admitted through the gates of the Holy City.

THE REPERCUSSIONS OF SEXUAL SINS UPON THE FORNICATOR

Simply by checking the references to fornication in the Bible, the effects of fornication upon the fornicator are clear.

DEFILEMENT

For out of the heart proceed evil thoughts, murders, adulteries, fornications, thefts, false witness, blasphemies. These are the things which defile a man...

Matt. 15:19–20

It is "from the heart" that defiling sin proceeds. Therefore, the writer of Proverbs, the Book of Wisdom, exhorts, "Keep your heart with all diligence, for out of it spring the issues of life" (Prov. 4:23).

How does one keep his heart pure?

> ...Give attention to my words; incline your ear to my sayings. **Do not let them depart from your eyes; keep them in the midst of your heart;** for they are life to those who find them, and health to all their flesh.
>
> Prov. 4:20-22 [EMPHASIS MINE]

"Defile" means to render unholy and to become unclean. It is the very opposite of holiness and sanctification.

> ...Beloved, let us cleanse ourselves from all **filthiness of the flesh and spirit**, perfecting holiness in the fear of God.
>
> 2 Cor. 7:1 [EMPHASIS MINE]

The inevitable consequence of defilement is the loss of fellowship with a holy God. "Pursue... holiness, without which no one will see the Lord" (Heb. 12:14). Are the fleeting pleasures of sin worth the forfeiture of our fellowship with God? May each of us be like Moses who chose rather to embrace the will of God "than to enjoy the passing pleasures of sin" (Heb. 11:25).

REPROBATE MIND

> God gave them over to a debased ["reprobate" KJV] mind, to do those things which are not fitting...
>
> Rom 1:28

In this context, sinners had become so sexually perverse and continued to "suppress the truth in unrighteousness" (v. 18), so that it is said, "God gave them up to uncleanness" (v. 24), and "God gave them up to vile passions" (v. 26). The Greek word for reprobate means "not standing the test," and signifies a mind so clouded by its own speculations that it is altogether unacceptable to God and, therefore, rejected by Him. It is a dreadful day when the convicting influence of the Holy Spirit is withdrawn and God decides, "My Spirit shall not strive with man forever" (Gen. 6:3).

DELIVERED OVER TO SATAN

There was a man in the Corinthian Church living in unrepentant incest with his father's wife. Paul instructed the church to exercise its disciplinary authority and "deliver such a one to Satan for the destruction of the flesh" (1 Cor. 5:5). The Apostle reminded them that "a little leaven leavens the whole lump. Therefore purge out the old leaven" (1 Cor. 5:6–7). This is in keeping with the instructions given by Jesus in Matthew 18 on how to deal with a sinning brother. After he has been confronted personally and then in the presence of two or three witnesses, his case is presented to church authority. Private admonition precedes public censure. If he refuses to hear the church, "let him be to you like a heathen" (Matt. 18:17). That is, he is deprived of the church's covering and communion, He must be considered as one belonging to Satan's kingdom rather than the Kingdom of God, and fellowship is withdrawn.

> "I wrote to you not to keep company with sexually immoral people... But now I have written to you not to keep company with anyone named a brother, who is **sexually immoral** — not even to eat with such a person"
>
> 1 Cor. 5:9,11 [EMPHASIS MINE]

"Christ has appointed this method for the vindicating of the church's honor, the preserving of its purity, and the conviction and reformation of those that are scandalous" (Matthew Henry).

A SIN AGAINST ONE'S OWN BODY

Sexual sin is a unique sin. It is unlike any other sin because "Every sin that a man does is outside the body, but he who commits sexual immorality sins against his own body" (1 Cor. 6:18). One might protest this argument by citing drunkenness and gluttony as sins against one's body, but fornication is different inasmuch as it gives the power of the body to another person. Fornication has an inherent depravity that defiles the "temple" purchased by the incorruptible blood of Jesus, making the fornicator's body one with the vile person with whom he sins. Thus, a demonic soul-tie is forged.

DESTRUCTION OF THE
FRUIT OF THE HOLY SPIRIT

Another passage where "fornication" occurs is in the listing of "works of the flesh" (Gal. 5:19–21). "Now the works of the flesh are evident, which are: adultery, fornication, uncleanness, lewdness..." These works of the flesh, unless they are quickly mortified, become demonic strongholds. Sowing to the flesh produces corruption (Gal. 6:8), and corruption (dead flesh) provides a banquet table for unclean spirits. Works of the flesh are the opposite of the "fruit of the Spirit" (v. 22–23); they cancel out the Spirit's fruit. Godly love is destroyed by sensual lust; Holy Ghost joy is replaced with fleeting pleasure, and the peace of God is drowned in fear of exposure and other fears.

CHRISTIAN TESTIMONY IS DESTROYED
THROUGH UNGODLY BEHAVIOR

"Therefore be imitators of God as dear children. And walk in love, as Christ also has loved us and given Himself for us, an offering and a sacrifice to God for a sweet-smelling aroma. **But fornication and all uncleannesss... let it not even be named among you, as is fitting for saints...**"

Eph. 5:1–3 [EMPHASIS MINE]

Each of us can name individuals, some who are prominent pastors and evangelists, who have lost the influence of a good testimony through sexual transgressions. Instead of the sweet smelling aroma of a godly witness, fornication causes one's influence to become a stench in God's nostrils.

Bringing Down the Wrath of God

"Let no one deceive you with empty words, for because of these things [fornication and uncleanness] the wrath of God comes upon the sons of disobedience."

Eph. 5:6 [Brackets mine]

Do not let the world deceive you into thinking you are missing something important because of your pure life style, or that fornication is somehow acceptable, or that you can sin without letting it bother your conscience. This is the devil's trap. Remember the angels "who did not keep their proper domain" (Jude 6), but left their own habitation to cohabit with women (Gen. 6:1-4), and remember Sodom and Gomorrah!

"God did not spare the angels who sinned, but cast them down to hell and delivered them into chains of darkness, to be reserved for judgment... and turning the cities of Sodom and Gomorrah into ashes, condemned them to destruction, making them an example to those who afterward would live ungodly..."

2 Pet. 2:4,6

Unrepented of and unforgiven sexual sin not only assures the transgressor of eventual Divine judgment, but it can also produce its own inherent judgment in this life.

"Can a man take fire to his bosom, And his clothes not be burned? Can one walk on hot coals, And his feet not be seared? So is he who goes in to his neighbor's wife; Whoever touches her **shall not be innocent.**"

Prov. 6:27–29 [Emphasis mine]

"And the men also turned from natural relations with women and were set ablaze (burning, consumed) with lust for one another, men committing shameful acts with men and suffering in their own bodies and personalities the inevitable consequences and penalty of their wrong-doing and going astray, which was [their] fitting **retribution.**"

Rom. 1:27, Amplified Bible [Emphasis mine]

GOD IS DISPLEASED

"For this is the will of God, your sanctification: that you should abstain from sexual immorality [lit. *fornication*]; that each of you should know how to possess his own vessel in sanctification and honor, not in passion of lust, like the Gentiles who do not know God; that no one should take advantage of and defraud his brother in this matter, because the Lord *is* the avenger of all such..."   1 Thess. 4:3-6 [BRACKETS MINE]

Sanctification means to be holy. Sanctification is being cleansed by the blood of Jesus and the washing of water by the word, and set apart for the glory of God. When God's Word says no man should "take advantage of and defraud his brother," it means not to overreach your brother by committing adultery with his wife.

For God did not call us to uncleanness, but in holiness. Therefore he who rejects this does not reject man, but God, who has also given us His Holy Spirit.   1 Thess. 4:7–8

The non-sanctified person is unholy, a vessel unfit for the Master's use. Thus, the fornicator disqualifies himself from being used by God. Instead, he serves the devil's purposes.

"Do you not know that to whom you present yourselves slaves to obey, you are that one's slaves whom you obey, whether of sin leading to death, or of obedience leading to righteousness?"
                    Rom. 6:16

CAUSES ONE TO DESPISE GOD

"For God has not called us to impurity but to consecration [to dedicate ourselves to the most thorough purity]. Therefore whoever disregards (sets aside and rejects this) disregards not man but God, Whose [very] Spirit [Whom] He gives to you [is] holy (chaste, pure)."

1 Thess. 4:7–8, AMPLIFIED BIBLE

Eli's sons "lay with the women who assembled at the door of the tabernacle of meeting" (1 Sam 2:22). Eli rebuked them saying,

> "'You make the Lord's people transgress. If one man sins against another, God will judge him. But if a man sins against the Lord, who will intercede for him?" (vv. 24-25).

God said of Eli's sons, "Those who despise Me shall be lightly esteemed" (v .30).

To reject God's commands is tantamount to despising and hating Him. God Himself said of those who disregarded His commandments,

> "I, the Lord your God, am a jealous God, visiting the iniquity of the fathers on the children to the third and fourth generations of those who hate Me."   Exod. 20:5

King David, in his prayer of repentance from adultery with Bathsheba, confessed,

> Against you, You only, have I sinned, and done this evil in Your sight...   Ps. 51:4

Sexual transgression is first and foremost against God — His law has been disregarded and He despised.

DEFILEMENT OF THE MARRIAGE BED[1]

> Marriage is to be held in honor among all, and the marriage bed *undefiled*: for fornicators and adulterers God will judge.
>
> Heb. 13:4 NAS [EMPHASIS MINE]

---

1 Also see *The Marriage Bed - Can It Be Defiled?*, Frank Hammond. Available at **www.impactchristianbooks.com**

LOSS OF KINGDOM INHERITANCE

> For this you know, that no fornicator, unclean person, nor covetous man, who is an idolater, has any inheritance in the kingdom of Christ and God.　　　　　Eph. 5:5

The consequences of immorality are serious! The inheritance spoken of is title to a future position.

> ...you were sealed with the Holy Spirit of promise, who is the guarantee of our inheritance until the redemption of the purchased possession...　　　　　Eph. 1:13–14

This inheritance cannot be claimed by the "sons of disobedience" (Eph. 5:6).

CAN LEAD TO FIRE AND EVERLASTING SEPARATION FROM GOD

> "The cowardly, unbelieving, abominable, murderers, sexually immoral [lit. fornicators], sorcerers, idolaters, and all liars shall have their part in the lake which burns with fire and brimstone, which is the second death."　　　　　Rev. 21:8 [BRACKETS MINE]

These are sinners, who through failure to repent and believe, cut themselves off from the Gospel benefits of forgiveness of sin and eternal life, which come "by grace through faith" in the Lord Jesus Christ.

REPERCUSSIONS OF SEXUAL SIN UPON MARRIAGE AND FAMILY

The seventh commandment, "You shall not commit adultery" (Exod. 20:14), represents God's protection for marriage and family. Ideally, the relationship between husband and wife should reflect Christ and His Bride, the Church.

> For this reason, a man shall leave his father and mother and be joined to his wife, and the two shall become one flesh. This is a great mystery, but I speak concerning Christ and the church.
>
> Eph. 5:31–32

Christ loves His Bride and washes her with the word.

> that he might present her to Himself a glorious church... that she should be holy and without blemish.   Eph. 5:27

Adultery destroys purity in the marriage relationship, and holiness "without spot wrinkle or any such thing" is negated. God is specific and zealous about the ways in which we are to reflect His Son. The "Rock" in the wilderness that provided water for three million Israelites was one example of Christ set for us. God instructed Moses to strike the rock with his rod which foreshadows Christ stricken for our transgressions through His crucifixion. Out of the Cross flowed the water of salvation. A little later on when the Israelites needed water, God instructed Moses to speak to the "Rock." Instead, Moses struck the Rock a second time.

This was an act of disobedience, for Christ only needed to be struck once to provide the water of life (thereafter all we need to do is to speak to Him in order to receive His blessings). Because Moses disobeyed, he was forbidden to enter the Promised Land. The husband/wife relationship, as a reflection of Christ and His Bride, is just as important and sacred as the "Rock" being struck once.

Adultery also violates the concept of "one flesh" created by the marriage union. Through sexual union with someone other than a spouse, one becomes joined to another person. Thus, a demonic soul tie is formed.

> Or do you not know that he who is joined to a harlot is one body with her? For "The two" he says, "shall become one flesh."
>
> 1 Cor. 6:16

Also, unfaithfulness in marriage wounds the innocent spouse. The the wound of rejection is compounded by betrayal. The sacred vow to "leave all others... until death do us part" has been broken, and the covenant of companionship has been destroyed. Divorce often follows. Jesus taught that adultery is the only legitimate reason for divorce.

> "...Whoever divorces his wife for any reason except sexual immorality causes her to commit adultery." Matt. 5:32

Divorce is not mandated where there is adultery, for there can be forgiveness and reconciliation. The divorce provision for adultery keeps a person from being bound hopelessly to a moral reprobate.

Where children are involved, the repercussions of sexual sin resulting in divorce are traumatic. There are endless hardships, painful readjustments and unresolved conflicts within and without.

TO SEE A SHORT VIDEO OF FRANK HAMMOND TEACHING ON THE REALITY OF SOUL TIES, AND HOW TO BREAK THEM, VISIT THE FOLLOWING WEBSITE:

www.impactchristianbooks.com/soulties

REPERCUSSIONS OF SEXUAL SIN UPON THE CHURCH

The latest statistics indicate that sixty percent of teenagers in evangelical churches are sexually active. In biblical terms they are committing fornication. There continues to be a stream of pastors, priests, evangelists and other church leaders exposed in sexual sin scandals. There are several that the author has been privy to that have not been covered by the media. These transgressions include adultery, homosexuality, pedophilia, prostitution and exhibitionism. Yet, little has been done to stem the tide or to restore the fallen.

The sin of incest was not being addressed in the Corinthian church. It was so flagrant a sin that Paul noted that it did not occur even among pagans. A man in the fellowship had either married or was living with his stepmother! Paul is reminded of the Old Testament prohibition that allowed no leaven in the Passover feast; leaven conveying the idea of evil or sin. Before the Passover was observed all leaven had to be removed from the house, for "a little yeast leavens the whole batch of dough" (1 Cor. 5:6 NIV). Similarly, the unrepentant sinner must be removed (excommunicated) from the fellowship; otherwise, the whole church would soon be affected. That is, others would take lightly the matter of sexual immorality and the church's standard of purity would be compromised. Sadly, this compromising attitude is prevalent today within church fellowships.

The church discipline called for is sadly lacking today in most congregations. Paul instructs the church,

In the name of our Lord Jesus Christ, when you are gathered together, along with my spirit, with the power of our Lord Jesus Christ, deliver such a one to Satan for the destruction of the flesh, that his spirit may be saved in the day of the Lord Jesus.

1 Cor 5:4–5

Excommunication removes a person from the benefits of fellowship. The members of the church are

not to keep company with immoral people... not to keep company with anyone named a brother, who is a fornicator... not even to eat with such a person.

1 Cor. 5:9,11

The phrase "not to keep company with" means not only to eliminate fellowship but not to have any social contact with such a person.

There is a twofold purpose in breaking fellowship with fornicators and other profane "brothers." First, one is to protect himself from identity with and contamination from such sinners, and, second, to shame the sinner to repentance so that fellowship can be restored. We learn from Paul's second letter to Corinth that the man has evidently repented, and Paul instructs the church to "forgive and comfort... reaffirm your love to him" (2 Cor. 2:7–8).

REPERCUSSIONS OF SEXUAL SIN UPON CHRIST

Of all the repercussions of fornication, the gravest of all is how Christ is affected by it.

> Do you not know that your bodies are members of Christ? Shall I then take the members of Christ and make them members of a harlot? Certainly not! Or do you not know that he who is joined to a harlot is one body with her? For "the two," He says, "shall become one flesh." But he who is joined to the Lord is one spirit with Him.
>
> 1 Cor. 6:15–17

Sexual relations represent more than a physical act; the two persons are joined together. Since the believer is already joined to Christ in a mystical union, the whole body is united with him. Thus, to join oneself in sexual union to another (outside of marriage) becomes the ultimate dishonor and reproach one can bring upon Christ. One Spirit lives and moves in Christ and His members! There can be no greater injury to our relationship with Christ than to indulge in sexual sin. There is no greater perversion of the divinely established marriage union than to join oneself to another through fornication. No wonder the apostle exclaims, "Flee fornication" (1 Cor. 6:18)

PORNOGRAPHY
ᴬ GATE ᴏꜰ
DEMONIC ENTRANCE

The Greek word for fornication is "*porneia,*" from which the English word "pornography" is derived. The term "pornography" comes from "*porno*" (prostitute) and "*graphy*" (write) that is, "the writings of a prostitute." The earliest written forms of pornography were the actual accounts of prostitutes, written by themselves or others, describing their escapades in sordid detail. Webster defines pornography as "the depiction of erotic behavior (as in pictures and writing) intended to cause sexual excitement."

Not only are the words "fornication" and "pornography" etymologically linked, the sin of fornication is rooted in pornography. It is a principal gate through which demons enter. We live in a time when Satan, "the god of this world," has led men to revise terminology in order to deceive. Those who are influenced by Satan choose terminology that tends to make evil appear acceptable and even righteous. Thus, pornography has come to be called "adult entertainment;" abortion is "terminating the pregnancy" and the place where unborn children are killed has become a "clinic." A discerning individual is not deceived by camouflaged terminology. A skunk by any other name smells the same!

Ephesians 6:12 tell us that our warfare is against "principalities." The demonic principality that rules over pornography is "the spirit of immorality," and it is linked with "the perverse spirit." From the Garden of Eden, God's purpose for sex has been procreation. Satan's objective is to pollute and destroy God's purpose by moving sexual expression

21

outside of God's boundaries and perverting it at every turn. Demonic powers cannot enter a man or woman unless the spiritual walls which God has placed to protect us are broken down.

Pornography opens the doors for demons to enter through the gate of the eyes. In order to guard himself against lust's temptation, Job set an example for all men to follow:

> "I have made a covenant with my eyes: Why then should I look upon a young woman?"   Job 31:1

Furthermore, Jesus taught us the necessity of guarding one's eye gate:

> "I say to you that whoever looks at a woman to lust for her has already committed adultery with her in his heart."   Matt. 5:28

Peter warns us,

> "The Lord knows how to... reserve the unjust under punishment for the day of judgment, and especially those who walk according to the flesh in the lust of uncleanness... having eyes full of adultery..."   2 Pet. 2:9–10,14

Most men and women who have allowed demons of lust to enter through the eye gate are oblivious that demons of immorality have entered their lives. Yet, those who either unintentionally or purposefully allow their eyes to gaze upon pornography have opened the gates for demons to enter. Once the demonic powers have entered, they stimulate their host to acts of perversion against God's laws of chastity. All believers who still struggle with recurring impure thoughts and mental pictures need to consider if their "houses" need to be cleansed of unclean spirits, even those that may have entered prior to salvation.

> Now may the God of peace Himself sanctify you completely; and may your whole spirit, soul, and body be preserved blameless at the coming of our Lord Jesus Christ.   1 Thess. 5:23

"Let everyone who names the name of Christ depart from iniquity. But in a great house there are not only vessels of gold and silver, but also of wood and clay, some for honor and some for dishonor. Therefore if anyone cleanses himself from the latter [vessels of dishonor], he will be a vessel for honor, sanctified and useful for the Master, prepared for every good work."

2 Tim. 2:19–21 [BRACKETS MINE]

Once a wicked spirit enters a life, it must be "cast out" (Matt. 10:1; Mk 16:17). The Greek word for "cast out" (*ekballo*) expresses aggressive action. It means to drive, expel or thrust out.

Sexual promiscuity and perverseness have become epidemic as pornography has increased. God's view of sexual expression has been replaced with body idolatry, where man worships the body rather than the God who created it. Obsession with the body and sex has led to fornication, adultery, homosexuality, lesbianism, bestiality, masturbation and unspeakable perversion.

Evidence is mounting daily that rape and child molestation are linked with pornography as men and women feed their minds and hearts on pornographic materials from television, movies, magazines, videos and the Internet. It is the author's conviction that divorce, extramarital sex, premarital sex, child abuse, molestation, sodomy and the murder of innocent lives through abortion is related to so-called sexual liberation, which results in disregarding and discarding the protective hedge that God placed around procreation. Apart from a spiritual awakening that reverses this onslaught of filth and turns us to the pursuit of righteousness, our nation is doomed.

Anyone who has worked in deliverance can testify that demonic spirits of sexual lust are common. Few have escaped their infiltration. We are now seeing lust's repercussions in the lives of our children and grandchildren. Sons and daughters are second-generation victims of neglect, living lives reflective of parents who have gone the ways of the world and abdicated their responsibility of bringing up children in "the nurture and admonition of the Lord" (Eph. 6:4).

Girls who grow up with memories of sexual abuse seethe with hatred of men and even God, for the Heavenly Father expects earthly fathers to reflect His love and holiness. Many women suffer horrible wounds due to betrayed trust. Rarely are these wounds addressed and healed. Many with deep psychological problems are victims of child abuse. Undoubtedly, most women identified with "women's liberation" organizations have been used or abused by men. They are filled with bitterness and hatred towards men, God, marriage and family. Unforgiveness and hatred give demonic powers a hold upon individuals who have been victimized either directly or indirectly by pornography's corruption.

HOW TO CONQUER SEXUAL SIN

"FLEE"

"Flee also youthful lusts; but pursue righteousness" 2 Tim. 2:22. The verb "flee" expresses continuous action. The fleeing of lust must be a lifetime discipline. Also, it is not enough to run away from wrong; we must also run after what is good. Timothy was to pursue righteousness, faith, love and peace. In other words, "Do not be overcome by evil, but overcome evil with good" (Rom. 12:21).

> "Flee sexual immorality. Every sin that a man does is outside the body, but he who commits sexual immorality sins against his own body."　　　　　　　　　　　　　　　　1 Cor. 6:18

The Greek word for "flee" is *pheugo,* from which we derive the English "fugitive." To flee temptation might be likened to a man escaping from prison; run as fast as you can! Run as Joseph did when he fled the temptation of Potiphar's wife.

> She caught him by his garment, saying, "Lie with me." But he left his garment in her hand, and fled and ran outside.
>
> Gen. 39:12

Peter prayed that we would escape the moral decay of this world:

> "That... you may be partakers of the divine nature, having escaped [*apophygontes*, lit. to flee away from] the corruption that is in the world through lust." 2 Pet. 1:4

Further, Peter warns against false teachers who

> "... allure through the lust of the flesh, through lewdness, the ones who have actually escaped from those who live in error. While they promise them liberty, they themselves are slaves of corruption; for by whom a person is overcome, by him also he is brought into bondage. For if, after they have escaped [*apophygontes*] the pollutions of the world through the knowledge of the Lord and Savior Jesus Christ, they are again entangled in them and overcome, the latter end is worse for them than the beginning."
>
> 2 Pet. 2:18–20 [BRACKETS MINE]

These false teachers speak of freedom from restraints of the flesh as some today speak of sexual freedom from all moral restraint. But these false teachers are themselves the slaves of depravity, for a man is slave to whatever has mastered him.

> Do you not know that to whom you present yourselves slaves to obey, you are that one's slaves whom you obey whether of sin leading to death, or of obedience leading to righteousness?
>
> Rom. 6:16

STRICT DISCIPLINE OF THE BODY

Paul illustrates the truth of body discipline with athletes who rigorously discipline their bodies in an effort to win an olive wreath, a gold medal, trophy cup or some other perishable prize. Christians have a far greater prize to gain.

> And everyone who competes for the prize is temperate [self-controlled] in all things. Now they do it to obtain a perishable crown, but we for an imperishable crown. Therefore I run thus: not with uncertainty. Thus I fight: not as one who beats the air. But I discipline my body and bring it into subjection, lest, when I have preached to others, I myself should become disqualified.
>
> 1 Cor. 9:25–27 [BRACKETS MINE]

A boxer in training beats the air by throwing out his arms, as the apostle puts it, to strengthen his arms and to practice striking a future opponent. There is no place for such behavior in spiritual warfare. Christians are ever in real combat. Our enemies are fierce and ever present. The discipline of the body calls for the curbing of fleshly appetites that war against the spirit man. The body must be made to serve the Spirit. "Beloved I beg you... abstain from fleshly lusts which war against the soul..." 1 Pet 2:11.

PUT TO DEATH FLESHLY LUSTS

> "So kill (deaden, deprive of power) the evil desire lurking in your members [those animal impulses and all that is earthly in you that is employed in sin] sexual vice, impurity, sensual appetites, unholy desires...
>
> Col. 3:5, AMPLIFIED BIBLE

The KING JAMES "*mortify*" means "to make dead" and is a very strong verb. It suggests not just mere suppression of control but complete extermination of the old way of life. "Slay utterly" expresses the idea more accurately. Macclaren, an author of Bible commentaries, likens it to a man who while working at a machine gets his fingers drawn between rollers or caught in the belting. Another minute and he will be flattened to a shapeless bloody mass. He catches up an axe lying by and with his own arm hacks off his own hand at the wrist. It is not easy nor pleasant, but it is the only alternative to a horrible death. So, the act of mortifying the flesh must be decisive and urgent.

It is impossible for us to move in opposite directions at the same time. Since we are to set our "minds on things above" (Col. 3:2), we must put to death or deprive of power our old ways of thinking and acting, thereby removing every enemy of spiritual growth and holiness. Fleshly lusts are to one's spirit what weeds are to a garden. They must be removed or else the good will never develop. This is our responsibility in response to God's grace.

POSSESS YOUR BODY IN SANCTIFICATION AND HONOR

> For this is the will of God, your sanctification: that you should abstain from sexual immorality; that each of you should know how to possess his own vessel in sanctification and honor; not in passion of lust...
>
> 1 Thess. 4:3–5

What is God's will for the redeemed? It is that we sanctify ourselves, cleansing ourselves of all filthiness of mind, speech and behavior, becoming completely devoted to glorifying God in our spirits and bodies.

1 Peter 3:7 refers to the wife as a "vessel" to be honored, so this is a plausible meaning of "vessel" in 1 Thess. 4:4. If one adopts this interpretation then it signifies that one should live with his wife in purity and honor. A wholesome marriage is Paul's antidote for "sexual immorality."

27

MAKE A COVENANT WITH YOUR EYES

"I have made a covenant with my eyes; Why then should I look upon a young woman?" (Job 31:1). The eye gate is the primary entrance of lust into one's life. The first recorded sin in the Bible began with a lustful look.

> So when the woman [Eve] saw that the tree was good for food, that is was pleasant to the eyes... she took of its fruit and ate.
>
> Gen. 3:6 [BRACKETS MINE]

David learned the hard way that a lustful look can lead to adultery; afterward he wisely made a covenant with his eyes, saying,

> I will set nothing wicked [base, worthless, naughty] before my eyes.
>
> Psalm 101:3 [BRACKETS MINE]

Today, that wicked thing looked upon can come through television, pornographic magazines, Internet pornography, lingerie catalogues, ogling a female or innumerable other ways. Jesus taught that the seventh commandment, "You shall not commit adultery," goes beyond the physical act. "Whoever looks at a woman to lust for her has already committed adultery with her in his heart" (Matt. 5:28).

Anyone who expects to keep his heart pure must guard his eyes which are entrance ways for uncleanness. Shame and a fear of exposure might keep a person from the overt act of adultery, but only a reverential fear of God will keep one from embellishing impure thoughts. Those who indulge their eyes in wantonness become allied to unclean spirits. All happiness, blessedness and spiritual inheritance are forfeited.

BE RENEWED IN YOUR MIND

... put off, concerning your former conduct, the old man which grows corrupt according to the deceitful lusts, and be renewed in the spirit of your mind, and that you put on the new man which was created according to God, in true righteousness and holiness.

Eph. 4:22–24

"Put off... put on... be renewed" are actions attributed to our own initiative. In other words, renewal is not automatic or synonymous with the new birth. Discipline is required. As believers, we now have the Holy Spirit dwelling within Who enables us to live a transformed life.

And do not be conformed to this world, but be transformed by the renewing of your mind, that you may prove what is that good and acceptable and perfect will of God.   Rom 12:2

WALK IN THE SPIRIT

I say then: Walk in the Spirit, and you shall not fulfill the lust of the flesh. For the flesh lusts against the Spirit, and the Spirit against the flesh; and these are contrary to one another, so that you do not do the things that you wish. But if you are led by the Spirit you are not under the law. Now the works of the flesh are evident, which are: adultery, fornication, uncleanness, lewdness...

Gal. 5:16–19

The flesh and the Spirit are in conflict. This is a never-ending battle, yet the Holy Spirit's residence within provides the power to overcome the evil desires of the flesh. Three synonymous phrases occur in this context which convey how we overcome by depending on the Holy Spirit: (1) "walk in the Spirit (v. 16); (2) be "led by the Spirit" (v. 18); and (3) "live in the Spirit" (v. 25). We as Christians are never free of the responsibility to choose God's bidding and depend upon His grace. Evil is overcome by yielding to the prompting of God's Holy Spirit. Paul is not talking about legalism, or adopting codes of dress and behavior, but a disciplined life based on obedience to the Spirit's urgings.

DELIVERANCE FROM SEXUAL SPIRITS

BE THOROUGH

Since the demonic kingdom sets up operation as a rank of spirits, a thorough deliverance is called for as opposed to an attack against a specific group of spirits or an isolated spirit. Rejection is usually a root issue with any sort of sexual problem. For example, rejection by one's father of varying degrees is found to be the root to homosexuality and lesbianism. Rejection deprives one of needed love and often opens a person to sexual lust in search of love.

GET TO THE ROOT

In ferreting out sexual spirits it is important to go back to the original gate through which such demons entered. Was the person sexually abused? Was he either molested or a molester? Was his first sexual experience masturbation or a sexual experience with another? The individual usually remembers his first sexual experience. This information will identify where the devil gained his initial foothold to build a stronghold.

The following is an overview of the steps and prayers that will lead you through the process of deliverance from sexual spirits and strongholds.

CALL UPON THE LORD

Confession & Prayer:

Lord Jesus Christ, I believe that you are the Son of God. You are the Savior come in the flesh to destroy the works of the devil. You died on the cross for my sins and rose up from the dead. You have promised in Your Word that, "Whoever calls upon the name of the Lord shall be saved." The Greek word for saved, *sozo,* means delivered! So, Lord, I call upon You to deliver me and set me free.

REPENT OF ALL SIN

Repentance of all sin is necessary for deliverance. God is a forgiving God. Confession of sin accompanied by repentance removes the devil's legal right.

Confession & Prayer:

I now confess all of my sins, known and unknown, and repent of each one. I ask You to forgive me and cleanse me in Your blood. I do believe that Your blood cleanses me now from all sin. Thank You for redeeming me, cleansing me and sanctifying me in Your blood.

Forgive All Others and Self

Forgive all who have abused and influenced you to sexual sin. It is also important to forgive oneself.

Confession & Prayer:

Lord, others have trespassed against me, but in obedience to Your command I now forgive each person who has ever violated me, seduced me or influenced me in any way sexually. As an act of my will, I now forgive (name them, both living and dead). Lord, I bless each of these. I love them with Your love, and ask You to forgive them also. And since You have forgiven me, I also forgive and accept myself in the name of Jesus Christ. The curse of unforgiveness has no more power in my life.

Burn your Bridges Behind You

Destroy — or restrict your access to — all books, magazines, video tapes, DVDs, computer websites and anything that has been used to fuel sexual fantasies and behavior.

BREAK INHERITED CURSES

Break inherited curses where there is sexual sin in the family history.

Confession & Prayer:

In the name of Jesus I confess all the sins of my forefathers, and by the redemptive blood of Jesus, I now break the power of every curse passed down to me through sexual sins in my family line. In the name of Jesus, I command every evil spirit inherited curse to leave me now.

BREAK DEMONIC SOUL TIES

Soul ties need to be broken with each sexual partner outside of marriage.

Confession & Prayer:

In the name of the Lord Jesus Christ, I now renounce, break and loose myself from all demonic soul ties formed through sinful sexual encounters. (Note: Be as specific as possible when breaking soul ties. Name each sexual partner and verbally renounce the tie with each one.) I accept God's forgiveness for each one. In the name of Jesus, I command all demons associated with perverse soul ties to go.

OBTAIN DELIVERANCE

Consult the list of sexual spirits (pages 41-43). Challenge each spirit identified, and command it to leave in the name of Jesus.

COMMIT YOURSELF TO CHRIST

Prayer & Confession:

Lord, thank you for forgiving me and delivering me from the guilt and bondage of sexual sin. I am your child, redeemed by the precious blood of Jesus. My heart's desire is to glorify Your name. In Your strength I will keep myself pure; and I will love, obey and serve You all the days of my life. Amen!

FILL YOUR HOUSE

Fill yourself with the opposite of whatever was cast out. Jesus warned that after deliverance one's "house" (life) must be filled so that the expelled spirits will have no opportunity to return (Matt. 12:43–45).

LIST OF SEXUAL SPIRITS

LUST OF THE FLESH

LUST OF THE EYES

FANTASY LUST

MASTURBATION

FORNICATION

ADULTERY

COMMON LAW MARRIAGE (SHACKING-UP); NO COVENANT; WITHOUT LEGAL SANCTION

INCEST

HARLOTRY, PROSTITUTION; SLUT; WHORE

RAPE; DATE RAPE; GANG RAPE

NAKEDNESS; IMMODESTY

INDECENT EXPOSURE

MOLESTATION; FONDLING

PETTING

LEWDNESS

HOMOSEXUALITY; SODOMY; ABUSERS OF THEMSELVES WITH MANKIND

EFFEMINATE MEN

CATAMITE (A BOY KEPT FOR PURPOSE OF SEXUAL PERVERSION)

LESBIANISM; MASCULINE WOMEN

LIST OF SEXUAL SPIRITS (CONT.)

TRANSVESTITE

ORAL AND ANAL SEX

ALL FORMS OF PORNOGRAPHY – WITH CHILDREN OR ADULTS; PICTURES, BOOKS & MAGAZINES; MOVIES & VIDEOS OR DVDS; INTERNET IMAGES AND WEBSITES

PEEPING TOM

PERVERSION

PARAPHILIA: A CONDITION IN WHICH A PERSON'S SEXUAL AROUSAL AND GRATIFICATION DEPEND UPON FANTASIZING AND ENGAGING IN SEXUAL BEHAVIOR THAT IS EXTREME. THERE ARE NUMEROUS PARAPHILIAS.

THE FOLLOWING ARE A FEW COMMON PARAPHILILAS...

(1) VOYEURISM: SEXUAL AROUSAL THROUGH OBSERVING UNSUSPECTING INDIVIDUALS WHO ARE NAKED, DISROBING OR ENGAGING IN SEXUAL ACTIVITY. ALSO, LISTENING TO EROTIC CONVERSATIONS (E.G TELEPHONE SEX).

(2) EXHIBITIONISM: PERVERSION MARKED BY INDECENT EXPOSURE.

(3) SADOMACHOSIM: GETTING PLEASURE FROM THE INFLICTION OF PHYSICAL OR MENTAL PAIN ON ONESELF OR OTHERS DURING SEXUAL ACTIVITY.

(4) PEDOPHILIA: AN ADULT'S SEXUAL FOCUS IS TURNED TOWARDS CHILDREN.

(5) TRANSVITISM: MALES DRESSING IN WOMEN'S CLOTHING.

(6) FETISHISM: FIXATION ON AN OBJECT OR BODY PART THAT IS NOT

PRIMARILY SEXUAL IN NATURE, E.G. WOMEN'S LINGERIE, HIGH-HEELED SHOES, SILK, LEATHER, FUR, LEGS, FEET, HAIR.

(7) NYMPHOMANIA: AN UNSATIABLE DESIRE FOR SEXUAL GRATIFICATION.

(8) APHRODISIAC: SUBSTANCE THAT AROUSES SEXUAL DESIRE OR ENHANCES SEXUAL PERFORMANCE.

(9) BESTIALITY (ZOOPHILIA): LYING CARNALLY WITH AN ANIMAL.

(10) DEPRAVITY.

(11) FRIGIDITY.

(12) OVERSEXED; UNDERSEXED.

(13) IMPOTENCE.

(14) OBSESSIONS (PARTS OF THE BODY).

(15) SEX ORGIES; SATANIC RITUALS; OCCULT SEX.

(16) ABORTION; MURDER; CHILD SACRIFICE (MOLECH).

(17) INCUBUS: AN EVIL SPIRIT THAT LIES UPON A WOMAN IN HER SLEEP, GIVING THE SENSATION OF SEXUAL INTERCOURSE.

(18) SUCCUBUS: A DEMON ASSUMING FEMALE FORM TO HAVE SEXUAL INTERCOURSE WITH MEN IN THEIR SLEEP.

(19) UNCLEAN DREAMS.

(20) BODY IDOLATRY; NARCISSISM.

(21) OBSCENITY; VULGAR SPEECH; BLASPHEMY; PROFANITY; DIRTY TALK.

(22) CURSES: BASTARD (ILLEGITIMATE BIRTH); SOUL TIES; VENEREAL DISEASES; REPROBATE MIND.

(23) GUILT: CONDEMNATION; SHAME; EMBARRASSMENT; SELF-HATRED.

(24) FEARS: GOD'S JUDGMENT; EXPOSURE TO AIDS, SYPHILIS, GONORRHEA, HERPES, & OTHER VENEREAL DISEASES.

Books, Booklets & Audio - Video

BY FRANK & IDA MAE HAMMOND

BOOKS

The Breaking of Curses

Comfort for the Wounded Spirit

Demons & Deliverance: In the Ministry of Jesus

A Manual for Children's Deliverance

Kingdom Living for the Family

Overcoming Rejection

Pigs in the Parlor

Study Guide: Pigs in the Parlor

Saints at War - Warfare in the Heavenlies

BOOKLETS

Confronting Familiar Spirits

Soul Ties

Repercussions from Sexual Sins

The Marriage Bed

Forgiving Others

Our Warfare

The Father's Blessing

God Warns America

The Perils of Passivity

Promoted by God

The Strongman of Unbelief

The Tales of Two Franks

Obstacles to Deliverance / Why Deliverance Sometimes Fails

DVD VIDEOS

The Schizophrenia Revelation

Breaking Demonic Soul Ties

Breaking Curses

The Wiles of the Devil

Obstacles to Deliverance

Binding the Strongman

The Mind, Will & Emotions

Deliverance from Self

Can a Christian Have a Demon?

COMPACT DISCS

The Deliverance Series (6 CDs)

The End-Time Series (6 CDs)

Faith Series (6 CDs)

Spiritual Meat Series (6 CDs)

Message on Love (5 CDs)

Freedom from Bondage (6 CDs)

Family in the Kingdom (6 CDs)

Walk in the Spirit Series (6 CDs)

The Church Series (6 CDs)

Recognizing God (3 CDs)

Available at www.impactchristianbooks.com

FRANK HAMMOND BOOKS

PIGS IN THE PARLOR*   0892280271

A handbook for deliverance from demons and spiritual oppression, patterned after the ministry of Jesus Christ. With over 1 million copies in print worldwide, and translated into more than a dozen languages, *Pigs in the Parlor* remains the authoritative book on the subject of deliverance.

STUDY GUIDE: PIGS IN THE PARLOR   0892281995

Designed as a study tool for either individuals or groups, this guide will enable you to diagnose your personal deliverance needs, walk you through the process of becoming free, and equip you to set others free from demonic torment. Includes questions and answers on a chapter-by-chapter basis as well as new information to further your knowledge of deliverance.

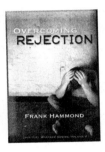

OVERCOMING REJECTION*   0892281057

Frank Hammond addresses the all-too-common root problem of rejection and the fear of rejection in the lives of believers, and provides steps to be set free. Learn how past experiences can influence our actions, and how we can be made whole.

THE BREAKING OF CURSES*   089228109x

The Bible refers to curses more than 230 times, and 70 sins that cause curses are put forth in Scripture. Learn how Curses are just as real today as in Biblical times. This book shows what curses are and how you may deliver yourself and your family from them.

A MANUAL FOR CHILDREN'S DELIVERANCE   0892280786

The Hammonds' book for ministering to children is a valuable tool for parents to learn how to set their children free from spiritual bondages. Learn the basics of how to effectively minister deliverance to children.

* Also available in Spanish

DVD VIDEOS

DVD TEACHING SERIES
BY FRANK HAMMOND

Frank Hammond amplifies and expands the teachings from *Pigs in the Parlor* in a series of Video DVDs. In these DVDs, he reveals additional truths gleaned from his far-reaching ministry in the area of deliverance and related fields. Much needed truths can be gained from his rich insights and down-to-earth teaching.

Watch excerpts now at:
www.impactchristianbooks.com/revelation

OTHER FRANK HAMMOND BOOKS & E-BOOKS

CONFRONTING FAMILIAR SPIRITS 0892280174

A person can form and develop a close relationship with an evil spirit, willfully or through ignorance, for knowledge or gain. When a person forms a relationship with an evil spirit, he then has a familiar spirit. Familiar spirits are counterfeits of the Holy Spirit's work.

SOUL TIES 0892280166

Good soul ties covered include marriage, friendship, parent/child, between christians. Bad soul ties include those formed from fornication, evil companions, perverted family ties, with the dead, and demonic ties through the church. Learn how you can be set free from demonic soul ties.

THE MARRIAGE BED 0892281863

Can the marriage bed be defiled? Or, does anything and everything go so long as husband and wife are in agreement with their sexual activities? Drawing from God's emphasis on purity and holiness in our lives, this booklet explains how to avoid perverse sexual demonic activity in a home.

FORGIVING OTHERS 089228076X

Unforgiveness brings a curse, and can be a major roadblock to the deliverance and freedom of your soul. Find the spiritual truths regarding the necessity of forgiveness and the blessings of inner freedom which result!

OBSTACLES TO DELIVERANCE 0892282037

Why does deliverance sometimes fail? This is, in essence, the same question raised by Jesus' first disciples, when they were unable to cast out a spirit of epilepsy. Jesus gave a multi-part answer which leads us to take into account the strength of the spirit confronted and the strategy of warfare employed.

THE PERILS OF PASSIVITY 089228160X

Some have made deliverance their ultimate goal in life. Deliverance is not a final goal, it is only a sub-goal on the way to fulfill God's purpose in life. God said to Pharaoh, "Let my people go that they may serve Me..." (Exod. 7:16). There is a purpose in God for each of us - and it is not passivity! Passivity is a foe – it will even block deliverance.

Miraculous Testimonies of
DELIVERANCE!

089228031X

POWER FOR DELIVERANCE - THE SONGS OF DELIVERANCE
BY BILL BANKS

This **book,** and also **e-book**, shows that there is help for oppressed, tormented, and compulsive people, and that the solution is as old as the ministry of Jesus Christ. From over 30 years of counseling and ministering deliverance, in the United States and abroad, Bill Banks highlights the common root causes of emotional and mental torment, and walks the reader through steps to be set free. Read numerous case studies of people who have been delivered from their torments and fears, including testimonies of over 60 spirits...

Drugs	**Anger**	**Cancer**	**Pornography**	**Perversion**
Fears	**Harlotry**	**Hatred**	**Witchcraft**	**Rebellion**
Cocaine	**Rejection**	**Temper**	**Occult Spirits**	**Childlessness**
Terror	**Torment**	**Suicide**	**Disobedience**	**Unforgiveness**
Smoking	**Murder**	**Bitterness**	**Homosexuality**	**Foolishness**
Sleeping Disorder		**Abuse of Women**	**& more!**	

Do Your Relationships Produce
Bondage or Joy?

Does someone manipulate you?
What are the symptoms of an ungodly relationship?
Are you tormented with thoughts of a former lover or friend?

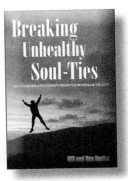

Breaking Unhealthy Soul-Ties
by Bill & Sue Banks

Unhealthy soul-ties involve the control of one individual over another, and can be one of the most difficult blocks to spiritual freedom. Some relationships are healthy and bring blessings into our lives; other types of relationships can bring demonic bondage to our souls. This book assists the reader in diagnosing both healthy and unhealthy relationships, and offers positive steps to personal freedom.

Impact Christian Books

THESE TITLES ARE AVAILABLE THROUGH YOUR LOCAL BOOKSTORE, OR YOU MAY ORDER DIRECTLY FROM IMPACT CHRISTIAN BOOKS.

Website: www.impactchristianbooks.com

Phone Order Line: **(314)-822-3309**

Address: **Impact Christian Books**
332 Leffingwell Ave. Suite #101
Kirkwood, MO 63122   USA

CPSIA information can be obtained at www.ICGtesting.com
Printed in the USA
BVOW11s1004281015

424000BV00018B/303/P

9 780892 282050